absolute *animal*

absolute *animal*

rachel dewoskin

the university of chicago press | chicago and london

The University of Chicago Press, Chicago 60637
The University of Chicago Press, Ltd., London
©2023 by Rachel DeWoskin
Published 2023
Printed in the United States of America

32 31 30 29 28 27 26 25 24 23   1 2 3 4 5

ISBN-13: 978-0-226-82905-0 (paper)
ISBN-13: 978-0-226-82906-7 (e-book)
DOI: https://doi.org/10.7208/chicago/9780226829067.001.0001

Library of Congress Cataloging-in-Publication Data

Names: DeWoskin, Rachel, author.
Title: absolute animal / Rachel DeWoskin.
Description: Chicago : The University of Chicago Press, 2023.
| Some poems in parallel English and Chinese.
Identifiers: LCCN 2023003041 | ISBN 9780226829050
(paperback) | ISBN 9780226829067 (ebook)
Subjects: LCGFT: Poetry.
Classification: LCC PS3604.E927 A64 2023
| DDC 811/.6—dc23/eng/20230124
LC record available at https://lccn.loc.gov/2023003041

♾ This paper meets the requirements of ANSI/NISO Z39.48-1992
(Permanence of Paper).

for my mom and dad

contents

absolute *animal*

anthrosphere

who brought toxic mollusks, boat or sneaker, human, vegetation,
     listen—cannibal snail, gravel, carbon, gibbon, bedlam—listen

to each sweet felicitation, to construction, our consumption. ravage, feast,
     ask any of the billion chickens toppling over its breast

how we make what's most delicious, ask the numbered, patterned cats, sleek
     past sense, sleek toward extinct, toward prowling cities, predators, one week

a lifetime for each chicken we invented. ask an ocean, rolled into a marble
     on the scientist's image: map of small blue trouble

{all the water covering earth's surface is thinner than the skin

of an apple} ask an apple, almond, lemon, olive, bouquet of kale
     ask *anthro* how it came to cover *bio*, fast slap, mat, plastic fat fail—

auditorium, kolkata's la martiniere school for boys, curious
     children fret about extinction. one asks, furious,

why grownups lie, asks: *why are kids the ones*
     you're asking for solutions?

     after each sheepish answer, boys shy as deer approach the stage, formal
          in their navy blazers, bravely handing scientists flowers {they'll

be strewn upon us, wilted, soon}. what used to be
     wild we've coaxed into our own. too hot, we

chill, too cold? heat up, too far we jet across, unpassable blast
     with dynamite so glittering our highways ribbon, silver tons of fish

float up into our open mouths. what might moor us back
     to earth, so much sweet water brackish, ask

fracked oil, ask detritus, whales, glaciers we are melting, melting into—

attention

the still, clear surface flickers, silver glint
of fish across ripples, a rising breeze
pushes a pattern {ribbon, moving print}
on river water quick, time, sideways trees

line cliffs so steep sometimes the vast trunks break
at night—fast popping, cracking, firework
claps, then quiet intense enough to make
us listen, slow down: foxes fuss, frogs lurk

in the singing dark, black bears and deer move
in circles of their own—societies
of fishing, teeth on fruit trees—swim above
the rapids with them, listen: blackberries

ripen, river mussels cling. try to hear
time {each fish} leap, flip, glimmer, disappear

the animal question

what's jumped from bird, bat, pig into us now:
sick thinking, we're upside down, disease
we know best and least, fever! ask bats how
we might relinquish all our certainties,

foremost among them, human boundaries—
but we created letters, numbers, all
the names for flus and animals, decrees
made powerful by shared belief—we fall

through wonder dark, nocturnal now, we are
such frail animals, vulnerable
throats open, we were singing, flew so far
infection melted us, unbearable

beauty is dangerous: whales, spiders, stars—
we made time, time made us, these hours? ours

sestina for the snake in a man-made lake

scaled head just above
the surface shattered when shot
by the bb gun a boy was teaching me not
to use but to love, *see?* when he fired,
i cried, shocked, concentric blood
on water gel-ish, dingy, ringing

shadow under a flipped boat, ringing
with his laughter, hard shell above
us, i laughed, too, the metal blood
smell of that boat stays like a snapshot,
visible, real, a 3d feeling, fired
from inside—some violence is not

easy to stop, to clock, to get, not
bullet, not venomous light, not ringing
leaves glimpsed from under a fiery
edge of rust, more like the boy above
me, skin hot, closed eyes lovely, shot
through: lashes, freckles, veins, blood

running under his lids and mine, blood
keeping us alive, combined, can we not
be here again, made new? give this a shot:
see forever, hear time bringing
us back, feel momentarily above
fear, young, the bristling world fired

iridescence up for us, the color of fire
a memory running through my blood,
in the marrow of this, submerged, not
bright red on the water, beauty ringing
in the distance still—here's a shot

in the dark—a trick shot
of the sort he fired

at the swimming snake ringing
the lake. in this version, its blood
still sprays, its scales explode, do not
sink but rise into a halo above

this place—i'm hiding here, boy, boat, blood,
gun, present tense a taste, glint, snake not
dead yet, not alive, just over, under, above

ways to love and leave you

trick question: do prairie voles love? they appear to
snuggle, breathe in sync, keep each other
close for reasons not efficient, not useful—
it isn't cold. whatever the paw, arm, fur, and patting
do, they will not make a baby vole, so why wrap
up and nuzzle? ask the meadow voles: those fuck
and flee or sleep, no staying the night, good luck
getting a next day text in the meadow, vole—
the prairie's where it's at if you want rodent love,
scramble the letters of your own name, or at least
fend hawks and weasels off {lusting to gobble your body}
with another vole close by. fear death? no need
to make too many sad comparisons here, i am already
at the airport, sky a momentary prairie i'll prance across,
taunting predators, hunting a like-minded vole {your loss}

social hour vole

the first prairie voles engineered to possess
genes from another species glowed green
{fluorescent jellyfish proteins}, let us read
out your bucktoothed burrower genomes—

what we found? you are not just rodent, not just
garden gobbling, fanged, or scrambling, but
more social than 97% of us. in fact, you're a hot
monogamous mammal, probably better at basic

interactions than i am post-plague lately. tell
me please, or better yet take over, glowing vole,
at my next obligation, cocktail party, small
talk conversation, just remind me how to roll

less like your slutty antisocial cousins, meadow
voles, who can't connect. what makes me
human anyway? the ways i love or don't or flee
or stay? test please, dye me useful, green, read away

when we say *they*

we mean the scientists, they

    mean north american voles, say

data taking shape indicates sweet

    rodents have perfected monogamy—

{scientific study language, seriously}

    marrying, building, renovating nests,

sharing parenting apparently completely,

    electrical probes attached to a girl vole's

brain buzz the medial prefrontal cortex

    and nucleus accumbens where the best

stored rewards get divvied after success,

    after she makes good choices {reliably}

romps only with a worthy vole, knows who

    that is, who merits monogamous huddling—*hey vole*

over there, you'll stay forever so come here—

    she's right is the thing. they pick each other the next day

and the next next next, day after day. say

    we play vole too, huddle away but our case

is at best an exuberant guess on the way—

hunt

fast approaching a vast void, the cat makes
a choice, leaps at the throat of a shadow,
almost bird, dream squirrel. all this kill takes
is imagination, moving so slow

our individual hairs ripple, rise,
we are waiting, stalking, tasting the play
of light on our tongues, our dilated eyes
squinting even at artificial prey—

the red lit stars of a neighbor's laser
let us dance along the edges of our
quiet confinement. these days for pleasure,
who needs what's real? just a little more

life, breath, leaping, a virtual catch or
something to pounce on, yes, stay lively for—

unseasonable

ladybugs on my windowsill, inside,
you twirl, red/black backs break into wings,
but there's nowhere to fly—you ought to hide,
it's snowing outside. flakes and vanishings

pin me. you pin me with your dumb parade,
bring back the sleek beetle i caught {sixth grade,
our teacher assigned bug collections, made
me cruel} soaking cotton in poison, i obeyed,

covered insects' faces, suffocated
them, stabbed their shiny shellacked bodies, cracked
thoraxes, knew something hurt but waited
until class to cry, when presenting facts

we all saw my halted beetle turning
on its pin, in pain i'm still unlearning

chemical peel

today I had the skin burned off my face for fun, to reveal one

beneath, a fresher girl, spring of last year instead
    of next. one more attempt to thwart the dead
        thing i'll be. my baby, five, paints me, red

        face, many creases, *where you smile,*
    she points, we laugh a while,
then she asks, *can mamu be my mama when you die?*

mamu's my mom, so it seems unlikely this will work. i say nothing true
    except that I will always be her mom. take this fake view:
        our nightly bubble baths will stay perpetual, i will shampoo

        her baby hair forever, although i know some truth somewhere
    someone once said something about it, time. it's hard from here
to put my finger on the moving circus in my mind. what's clear:

girls fly, swing, dip, turn days to magic, lemon candy,
    chapter books and princesses, neytiri, avatar, ballet,
        bright broccoli in the trash, i cherished that first lie,

        my baby, three*: how did that get there anyway?*
    And actually who can say?
what was my great-great-grandma's name?

will my babies' babies' babies remember one syllable
    of my babies' names? dalin and light, unthinkable,
        the letting go, sing such slow vanishing, hold on to each pink bubble

taxidermy

elk out our car window

you are all eyelashes, heels, neck tag a shimmery jewel,

glamorous gaze impossible to catch, your head and neck

shift, watch, wait, blink—

you stand between trees lovely enough to carry off and drape with ornaments

at any moment. in the grand hotel lobby, what are they—ferrets? muskrats? weasels

of some sort poke from a basket mounted on the wall, one duck's wings

open onto fourteen whiskered heads and twenty-eight resin eyes,

hard necks, snouts frozen above a christmas tree

like this one but shot through with tinsel, scattering

slivers of shrapnel, flickering fireplace stacked with fake gifts,

its stones warm as whatever ran down the canyon walls—

here, traces of those hunts are covered by snow into which your hooves press

star prints, each gesture crisp and sure, each breath still visible

i will see you for years of winters, again and again, each time

my daughter lies down and waves

her arms and legs, making an angel

heathkit tv 1980

what my father made and gave me, nouns:
    transistor, fastening, capacitor. he was a sort

of sorcerer, wizard at building, his mind
    a sleek machine of memory, rebuilt

from youthful chaos and some suffering
    we didn't discuss, just fixed into a different

tense. the five of us, assembled, 1980,
    rendered late, again: my mother, brothers,

stars are moving on a screen my father took from
    separate components, fused, they dance, laugh, entertain,

reflect us, lit up swing sets, sunsets, tv sets, antenna,
    current, plug, each piece makes another work. hot spark

of a soldering gun connects by melting; he is always
    working, making what we need to see. we move

from planet to electric planet, apple 2e joy, invaders
    tick atari basement aliens we shriek at, shoot

up, 2d childhood, sweet summary of super glue
    and batteries: he has a fix for anything we break. i'm

sick this year, my voice back young again, some fear:

        dad? can you help me for a second here?

we're all grown up but i am not immune
    to what's most fragile in me or the story at his stories' cores:

that we will be okay, that he'll make sure—
    this fix needs a tricky switch flipped back to who we were {a cure?}

my dad's socially distant heart surgery

the loopy hours might bring on a haze—
a little delusion, no sweat! they said.
the doctors called *abnormal thinking* days
after this surgery *normal.* instead

of trying for reason, let's imagine this:
a heart rebuilt, bionic, powerful,
mom on the screen now, blowing him a kiss,
his voice: *what fun it is to have people*

who turn you over, walk and feed you, we
should try out new procedures when we're home—
the nurse is laughing while machinery
plays beeping, chilly notes—she serves him some

lime jello, virtual, neon, green bright
and distant as last summer's lost sunlight

his meds

every iambic pharmaceutical:
warfarin, aspirin, amiodarone,
such magic pressed in tablets {sensible
of what the normal range is, in the zone

of hope, of realism, of our hearts;
we count the beats, meds, many days between
replacements, new repairs, bionic parts}
what can't be measured: from what we have seen

to what we may or may not see from here—
is pulse a lineage? inheritance?
what order from this chaos, primal fear?
please, coumadin, thin opposite of chance,

calm his blood, my blood, certainly let it not
run quick—or slow—or thick enough to clot—

arrhythmia

my god we learn hospital language fast
what's atrial, cardiac, filial,
quick fibrillation, valve, root, arch, way past
our pay grade here, sick, upside down until

we spring you from this place that's saving you,
thus saving us, cut into *what*? replace,
repair, slow blood down, wait! soak up what's true
slowly, this truth may pitch us into space

so terrifying we can't return. what else
is there but you, laughing, saying they froze
then thawed your body, brought back slow each pulse
a hundred years we waited. how to close

a sternum, stanza, suture, layer, wound?
measure something like love, abstract, fine-tuned

feel it if

if train, if leaving

    is what you are

doing, gear up, buck up, chin up you

    fuckup, this all comes of not saying what

      you want, need, nary a difference

        there, come here, why if you loved

    in outward ways did all those furious words

      stay in your marrow,

why electric tracks   why throw yourself   why death as finish line

    comeuppance   why didn't you put

      language outside, everywhere, say everything, if only—

      if what is dust is actually in fact a fly

on the windowsill,   one wing

    crushed, the other veined and active,

      flapping, pumping, if a body spins,

      pinned down, if incapacitated, smashed,

      if now arrives,   what then,   you see?

these days i keep falling

i keep falling. slipped on the rocks in a river and caught
my left pinky, landing, tore bone away {*avulsion*}, thought
it would heal, was wrong, did not. i am not distraught
though, change is falling, change this year has taught

me: kick harder in sleep, remember falling may prepare
us to fall harder, faster, be broken, okay, i won't despair—
blading uphill, i slipped and cracked a rib right where
the incline sharpened, errant twig or seedpod there

lodged in my wheel, twisted, flipped me over, numb
with shock. i'm not distraught, this fight is different from
the one i used to have with my body. i've become
myself descending, protective of what i opposed, some

version i'm working to save, someone who
is falling and climbing through time—and you?

back

wildfire's fingers comb the mountains
where my family, young and hopeful, now spends

summers. this year's different, the salmon
river's salmon are in danger, though they swim and

we swim, too, in water hot and toxic

burning is visible at night, orange tracing
crests of trees, alive, flames racing

into laundry on the line, cracked pine cones, so much

ash and time. last night
i dreamt i poured cement
into his empty socks and
he rose, statue from a gesture—
we were still young, still in beijing then

i woke knowing again he's gone, his thoughts just river
rocks that clatter, knock, and falter—i remember

what dead is each time—no longer him, not me, no
sleep, don't slip, do not let go

of his hand on the steering wheel that night, single

headlight, smoke. i am
alive, if not for him,
would I be burning, too, then,
now, in a broken car on fire, when?
we spent our twenties engulfed. birds circle

here in california, patient carrion, fear

guides me back to vanished years, beijing

        city bright with youth
        i loved, neon billboards,
        alleys, echoes of his pulse
        in my hands, mouth, chest, his wingspan
        vast, not the freezing

hospital garage. unlit cement layers of cars
and his mother, so small, all of nothing coming at her—

II.

once before he died we climbed a mountain, one star
shot across the sky, gorgeous with laughter,

        but now i'm here in a clear green river

           watching american fire,
           ten years later, as far
           from beijing and from then
           as nature, as hotshot fighters
           who drop from helicopters, beat fire

back by starting more fire. i live hours we
work to beat back by stacking more hours, too, i see

time close behind me all the time, another new way
to find he dies again, 1999, his body

        underneath a harley belt and jeans

           is lost {so much} were we
           real at all?   and if
           so   so what—i grew up, left,
           came here, where, home? planned these

augusts, year after year swerving through burning trees

estrangement

in 1999, american planes flying for nato in yugoslavia bombed the chinese embassy in belgrade. america called it "a tragic mistake." chinese students rioted in beijing.

*

our ambassador ate freeze-dried ice cream,
trapped astronaut in an embassy basement

hiding from riots while molotov time took us
by hideous surprise and now nobody's about

except me,
losing my vocabulary

*

it tastes like winter on the street
at 3 a.m. it's always

today in beijing, yesterday
in the west. you and i were tie-dyeing

shirts at "five colors earth," spinning pottery, too—
when the demonstrations began. here, a new

barricade blocks my courtyard. i climb, twist
my ankle, sit a minute thinking of your hips,

often sharp against mine, your zipper
you once called an access site, *like*

at the great wall, it makes me laugh
every time, such fun for tourists like me

*

this was a foreign policy decision
your america made, you propose. i slip

into something less miserable than english:
silence, don't say *not mine, not mine,* back

at the embassy i can't see
what is happening until I see you

throwing something. you are frozen,
holding something, throwing something

what are you holding, throwing? you see
me, explain: *i came to rubberneck, see what's up* —

you pass your banner to a friend, drop rocks,
your sign in his hands reads: **"down with naot"**

it's nato, i say and float away, this city
wasn't mine but youth confused me, you

have made something from english and not
asked me to proofread, silly, i know, but

so painful all the same that i can't make anything
except broken chinese letters to you, i do not

write the story i owe an american paper
i don't know what the story is. can i

promise this impossible thing
please: that you will be my only reader,

and everything i'll make from here
will be a question?

burn this translation

poem on returning
by he zhizhang

回鄉偶書
賀知章

少小離家老大回
鄉音無改鬢毛催
兒童相見不相識
笑問客從何處來

left home so young, came back old
dialect unchanged, hair bald
the kids i see see me, call
where are you from? somewhere far

on the eve of government exams to secretary zhang

by zhu qingyu

七言绝句 近试上张水部
朱庆余

洞房昨夜停红烛，
待晓堂前拜舅姑。
妆罢低声问夫婿，
画眉深浅入时无。

out go the wedding chamber's candles
tomorrow the bride faces your parents—
finished preparing, she asks only
did I paint my eyebrows on okay?

climbing white stork tower
by wang zhihuan

登鸛雀樓
王之渙

白日依山盡，
黃河入海流；
欲窮千里目，
更上一層樓。

the white sun ends in mountains,
yellow river flows to sea;
to view the end of infinity,
climb one more level and see.

halfway

by li bai

半渡上遼津
黃雲慘無顏。
老母與子別
呼天野草間

halfway across this fording
clouds grieve colors fading.
mothers with war-bound children
weep from fields to heaven

drinking alone under the moon
by li bai

月下獨酌
李白

月下獨酌
花間一壺酒，
獨酌無相親；
舉杯邀明月，
對影成三人。
月既不解飲，
影徒隨我身；
暫伴月將影，
行樂須及春。
我歌月徘徊，
我舞影零亂；
醒時同交歡，
醉後各分散。
永結無情遊，
相期邈雲漢。

from a wine jug among
flowers, i pour myself some,
raise to toast the moon;
face shadows that make
us three friends. moon has
no wine, just shadows
follow me—this moment
of closeness brings joy
that should last until spring.
moon waves, and I sing,
dance, my shadow wild,
not crazy until
i'm drunk, alone until
we meet again, stars.

snapshots of what's called for

the dead have ground
    to a halt. already, they are forever
        mixing messages, insects in
            their sockets. take stock
              of what is lost:

              words that rose up, heliumed o's floating moonward,
           so many lovely spirals twisting into the logic of our lineages.
        my grandma said that guests who stay too long begin
      to smell {like fish}—she made gefilte fish herself
by hand, sliding bones out the bodies

of live whitefish who'd flapped water
    on our bathtub walls. she said, *their time is up,*
        and i saw it shimmering above us,
            its glittering scales iridescent, repetitive

            nights crack under the weight
              of their own smiles, fanged light
                of the stars holding tight
                  until from their great height
              they plummet, shooting across
            dark streaked with loss

            lobster is hot on a white plate
              we wear bibs of its cartoon life around
                our necks, hold the silver sound
                  of shell cracking and wait
              for meat to slide out, slim
            forks moving into each bright limb

where are we? in an in-between,
    the heat of being
        alive welds walls, the ceiling meets the floor,
            compressing us into what's called for:
        our finer selves, connected to those who tell
      us we are mothers, fathers, children, lovers, everyone fading back
like slides catching fire, edges curling, blooming, burning black

some girls

maybe malaria made us delirious, or else
    what strange history took place?   i was,
no, wait, not *was* but *had*, the pulse

of a corpse. we landed on an island where
    we died of thirst   no, wait—
it wasn't thirst, we drank some water

what it was—we starved for years
    such skinny misery, our twenties   before i was
this me, the one with girls i grew, i was my body

every day so suddenly another yesterday time stacked
    the dark into a line of heart attacks,   blue panic
air-popped popcorn, water, track

of running, pounding, all of nothing coming at me
    constantly   dear faint girls,   i drove that highway
too, that's not control. houses, fields, all those trees

and objects not us, stuffed, our cars devoured fuel, road, yellow
    lines we blew by animals so fat and lucky   to be full:
impossible *do not, do not, do not, you're not* a hollow

voice, my voice, dear girls like me, i know the sound
    of *please erase me*   and the flesh always   left to mock
our work {there's never skeleton enough}, try this: to be someone

worth love, a baby, say   your own,   your mom's,   a mom
yourself sit, eat, digest   hush the tempting   clatter of bone
that wants to be exposed for one slow moment let your body be   home

dressing

i'm a clown because whatever i put on becomes a gown
      anyway, and this is the breast guy, so i'll keep my pants on
          {mercy, but what pants?} no shirt or bra though, so i don't want
             underwear visible above my waistline, don't want
      too high-waisted or he'll have to fuss with buttons
          to check my stomach, my stomach, don't imagine
             what he might be finding, turn my mind's volume
                low as it goes, must have socks or perish from fear,
          he starts with my wrists, runs his thumbs along veins,
       what wrong blood in those, so close to thin bones? i hate tights,
    constricting, cutting off, what if i run, slip? a button-down shirt
  means no pulling, no ripping earrings off on the way, pearl choker although it hurts
to unclasp and hide those in my purse, he checks my neck
  and collarbone, rib after rib. if the shirt is tight, i'll be shellacked
    with panic, don't want to be slick, don't want to think,
        nothing baggy or callous or frivolous. excessively formal
           might tempt smiting: who do i think i am, a doctor myself?
             not safe: seams up the backs of stockings, heels,
      but flats make me short and more afraid, i can't bear terrible news
    in sneakers or anything a little legging-like, sleepy sweats, pajamas,
jeans? no way. i don't want to be real. wait, i want to be real,
    to be me even on this day, today, when my sensitive
      oncologist might meet my eyes with concern in his,
        professional hands may articulate a dangerous shape,
          lump, tissue shifting, if he says *concern*—maybe a raincoat,
        wings, waders for fishing, plastic up my thighs, can i
      go goth, protect with chains, locks, hold my chin up?
  nope. i picked silk shorts, ribbonlike belt tied tight to distract
from the one on the gown. and the news? was good today, it was
  good, it was good, did i hear you right, did you give
      my life back for six months, let me float to the other side
        of this equation, *you can get dressed now*—
          a woman in the waiting room as i emerged said, *you look*
      beautiful {she was still at the beginning of fear}. i said, *so do you.*
    it was true, blue dress, soft boots, open coat about to be that gown,
  i wanted to add, *you'll be okay, he won't say* concern, *won't send you to terror town*

to every day a new machine, fresh, next needle, report, soft something scan, your cells
turning, back to where fear is queen, but even leaving,
what power did i have? so we just looked at each other, she fastened
her wrist tag on, patient, as i rode down and out, to shriek
relief down icy streets as hard and fast as jewels, glittering invincibly,
okay this time, okay, did i dress for that to undress for this,
kind oncologist, please cure my nightmare vulnerability. must we be
peeled, even to be? see you in six months, we'll see.

let me be

a sunflower instead, thirsty face pressed against the sun, let me be bigger than every
other stalk in the garden, let me be not in a garden but wild, giant, omnipotent, let me
take up more light than i need, want, deserve, more, more than any other cluster of petals can
grab or soak first, i'll block and gobble it all, let will be my reason/appetite be my will, i am
not saying i'll choke both the dainty apologists and competitors out on purpose, just that i am
outside time, finished with niceties, crazed with light, with wonder as rage, or maybe it's only
i'm no longer me {have been let be}, now too full of scalding sunshine to get out of the way

vanity

naked lately my body may
      be medical. black bathrobe butterfly
          is a sudden paper gown,
              shuddering open, out
          the window of this noiseless room, society
      i no longer inhabit happening. i'm someone i am not, want to fly
high above my life on wings or strings i'm making
      in my mind. what's this, old age? to the doctor taking

blood, i say we've all been ancient before,
      aware of what we can't know, so much more
          than what we can, good veins are what
i'm good at. move, change, be the move, the change. shut
      up please, cells, listen to the needle. each certainty's a joke, each
          tense arrives regardless, future's here, new mark on my face
          a mystery: why, face?

why make what hates you, what you hate? which cell
      turned strange, against me and our interest? {unclear}. what will
          the docs take, which pieces will they replace with artificial
              parts {picture a rabbit my dad once got me at the circus, inflatable}
      this body's still mainly mine, and what's real anyway, what i kept or gave
              away? what makes us, what we lose or save?

      where i am at night, the foxes scream
          in human tones, *mom mom mom mom mom mom*, i turn,
              yes? but every angle hides surprises i created
                  and forgot. each morning flips the mirror around to face
                  the wall, reflect nothing at me,
              hush mirror, hush mind, eyes, avert yourselves, be
                elsewhere, please, there's nothing here to see—

a surgeon sawed me open, sewed me up

each thought begins with *here* and then it moves

    across the flat midwest or china, loves

displacement, opposites and magnets, back-

    spaced pages, lines, erase, revise, run, track

each gesture—let me flee and still remain

    intact—contain my life, please, poem, contain

my bones, so fragile now. what difference does

    is everything. i *am* difference, i was

before the surgeon light and steel too—

    i had many versions to believe. you

are relieved i woke up me, didn't die, won't

    yet, something else will do us part, so don't

try to keep me. here, instead, *all aboard,*

    let's go! my mind conducts us forward

time falls like ice our fridge makes, floor

    buckling under so much melting, more

ice chips please. *please rest*, you beg, but revving,

i am chewing cold, my stinger poised, buzzing

with wonder, am i doubled? halved? just rearranged?

while {i was} writing this, everything changed—

double body, hot lasagna

decades of mornings strung, popcorning
a festive line, not twisted yet, still linear, so stop mourning
what you've yet to lose, weeping for girls not grown
up, old, done, done for—you are always around
the next bend, just ahead of panic, as if preventing
each terror by predicting or wishing, inventing
order? dusting, mopping, grieving, you are chaos at its core, you
are, and married also to yourself. rhyme's never new
enough to change the basic shape of questions too
tricky for deft analysis, say what? till death, in hot complexity, you do
vow such abundance, question scale, decorate your naked self: lipstick,
eyeshadow, lashes black as something burnt, one trick
in your deck is singing two babies back to sleep
at once, awake yourself, making promises no one can keep:
it'll be okay, there, there, bake decades, iambs, lasagna, too,
to a crowd of selves, stay true
to a crowd of selves, stay true
it'll be okay, there, there, bake decades, iambs, lasagna, too,
awake yourself, make promises no one can keep:
sing two babies back to sleep,
eyes closing, lashes black as something burnt, one trick?
vow abundance, another? question scale, decorate with lipstick,
stay tricky with deft analysis, till death, in hot complexity, you'll do
enough to change the basic shape of questions too
close to see clearly, stay married to yourself. rhyme's no new
order, still, rhyme, dust, mop, grieve, be chaos at its core. you
can live each terror predicting and wishing, inventing
next bends, keeping ahead of panic, preventing
the done in done for. you are always around
what you've yet to lose, girls not grown
up, still yours, a festive line glittering, so stop mourning
decades of mornings strung, popcorning

taunting the turkey vultures with love
{a golden shovel for gwendolyn brooks}

we dove off cliffs, down, down while birds rose above, itched

and circled, waited, lost us to life. ha! you and i were made instantly

lively by the cool river, driven, shot through with silver beneath

a bubbled narrative, opposite death, more like ongoing wonder
among the

many fast fish who sliced by. is this how it feels to float up nourished,

laughing, the fingered wings of carrion vanished? the sky is a promise, sun
skull white

tiny staples

turns out chronic terror is our shared core—
count cars on the drive {so few}, more
comfort in whatever we might sanitize:
hands, gloves, masks, mail. freeze

each other out, heat up this planet we've
been ravaging, forgive us? final apple eve
forgot to wash, so dangerous, so delicious she
could not resist the living, asking part, and we

can't either. okay, so, bread's rising, sun
hangs high, a glowing prop someone
made for a horror movie, silver clay
lightie shapes into small mice each day

we make more tiny staples: clay plates,
mini fruit {cherries, apples}, knives, forks, rates
suddenly exponential, death! we're finished
with familiar, stable, safe. diminished,

i make rollerblades for mice. nothing
cures anything. we are collective wishing
are what we'd mostly stopped noting,
lived with the sweet sense of forgetting—

once, we were inured: hot hug from someone
not my own, strangers' names on my tongue,
maybe yours, reason the need to be 3d, be done
with stillness, see my parents, feel a season

shift, shape days, *hi, mice,* all we don't know
sometimes incapacitates and suffocates us, go,
go, clay car i made today! flee! drive fast
down vicarious streets, get us past this—

fear

today although there's light outside

we're under something, all of us on a ride

half unsurvivable, uncertain, unconscious,

shivery, chilled, we quiver, whisper, *hush*

little baby. whoever tells you not to cry

is sleeping with an open eye—

chance, chicago

what bagels and bouquets of kale do in a bath i'm
learning/dancing/half-dressed/mambo no. 5/my kitchen
is designated tetris spaces: contamination station,
soap station, rinse station, dry station, every jam

jar sprayed, surface of each lettuce leaf clean, an outside
chance i know, but risk's expansive. is one sun hot enough
to burn this off, away from us, are we us, are we tough
or broken, are we what we eat, wash, shrink from, hide

inside ourselves? or safe? strange groceries stack and gather,
repeat, vanish, remake patterns, remake us, these new days
take tiny shapes, then slip and fall away, become ways
lives narrow into—stop. points of light on the lake. i'd rather

lick you, raise our arms in a stadium wave, take
the opposite of a distanced risk, touch everything, but now
chaos disorders wonder. letters, stanzas, rhyme, somehow
let this city sparkle, please. at eight each night, people make

a constellation, shine flashlights out our windows, some
solidarity in those bright dots, man-made stars, say *hello,
i see you.* we'd never have met, but here we are, a show
of company, south loop a momentary escape from

lonely. pilsen, bronzeville, hyde park, flashing *stand
with me for a second*, thinking: maybe we'll find something
unlike shared terror, past surviving all we clean, catch, bring.
chicago blinks in sync for a second, light carries, let it land—

sunset/sonnet

sometimes we're back to raw meat, the red slap
on a cold table, white plate, bedsheet, fact:

    when we have nothing, we can't sing
    of much, since each thing

needs *like*, that hard sharp tooth
to press words up against, define, that's me for you,

        that's us, gobbling love, swallowing sorrow.
        is knowledge what we keep or borrow?

    i will always hear your voice after the baby, gone,
    was bathed, dressed, photographed, buried. on

        the phone you said, *grateful*, said, *held him*, take cover,
        but how? can't feel this, can't feel forever horribly never over,

    you knew, i knew, we both knew we know
              nothing but what we feel {cold shadow}

airplane landscape, 1992, true story

heading west were forty-six babies, crying sirens, row
    after row of tiny people propped on airline logo
        pillows, strapped with seat belts, plane a cartoon
            of cuteness, cooing, napping, looking about. soon
        so many separate lifetimes never intersected again, of course,
    as strange as strangers are in flight, but nighttime came before we took off

and i held a baby because she cried, because a flight attendant said yes when
    i asked, also the woman from an agency said please, so we women
        all took babies, made awkward jokes. i held that girl for
            twenty hours, the longest I had ever held another person, more
        time stretched into years, into clouds, into the way
    that soothing my daughter born fifteen years later gives me that baby

back sometimes. on a plane on her way somewhere unknown,
    hum, roar, *there there baby*, hot jolt of an engine,
        the only comfort for a frozen sky and world passing out the window
            were the lullaby of her weight, warmth, mouth a lovely o

landing

the airplane punted, shooting straight back up
in wind so wild it made us go solid,
falling, screaming, praying: *please interrupt*
our deaths, god, pilot, help, attendants did

what we have always waited, feared, watched for:
collapsed, sobbing, let their carts go smashing
into the galley, watched small bottles pour
forth alcohol like blood, we were crashing—

but we evened out, silence a shape in
front of, hanging over our aborted
deaths, how many extra lives had we been
granted? p.a., pilot's voice reported:

some weather in chicago, we would hold
this pattern {into stories we all told}

dream view from above

asleep, i was a bird, shocked queen
  of my own feathers, wires, spells, a spleen
    outside my body, i asked, beak chattering,
      what's internal? maybe i'll sing

about what can be put out, *put out*, i flew,
  valedictorian of everyone i knew
    in a town below me, eating,
      euphemistic bullshit competing
        for truth, from their mouths came words
        even we birds

found worrisome. i woke the day
  you had to end a pregnancy,
    loved you, took you to the clinic in new york, stared
      at carpet for six hours, my eyes dared
        to make meaning in its swirls, but my arms
        flapped, helpless. what harms

us most? women
  live brutal moments woven
    into patterns we'd unweave if not for
      all we're in {time, scaffolding, this/that trap}, also, more
        than time, can we please change
        the factories of ourselves, rearrange

    what meaning is, stop squinting all
      the time at what we have to make and take?
        turn animal—

your death

i dropped the spoon we brought

from your place in new york, hoped

to have you always in our kitchen—

was i cooking, talking, spinning when,

wooden, it shattered weirdly, elephant

handle in bits, *don't be superstitious*,

i said, although alone, *it's coincidence*.

there are too many ways to tell each story:

what you taught seemed always inexpressibly

hard won, prison, redemption, i was the easy

beneficiary. now, how to ask this last question:

where are you, are you okay? insane,

i know. i watched you go. you there, not

there, face turned toward what boundary?

once you, you went empty. what's a body? today

such brief sun from under a gray layer,

how your ashes stayed still in strange air, hovering

above a river we stood over before blowing away so slow

they vanished into everywhere, now visible somehow

tenacity

pearls, you outlasted her, as if you marked

    the seasons of a twice lived,

raucous life, or more you were that life,

    around her softening neck, nacre, advice

against the chaos of decay—

    were you flung bedside or left on while music played away?

it's clear what came to pass, what happened anyway,

    strung now around my neck, as you are, every day

acknowledgments

my deep gratitude to anne carson, robert currie, christine jones, randy petilos, alan thomas, garrett kiely, robert pinsky, rosanna warren, kirun kapur, fred speers, jill grinberg, elise paschen, simone muench, thea goodman, julia hollinger, lara phillips, donna eis, raisa tolchinsky, william zhang, suzanne buffam, chicu reddy, and my beloved comrades in writing, reading, organizing, and hoping: writers for democratic action's askold melnyczuk, siri hustvedt, robin davidson, carolyn forché, tara skurtu, paul auster, sophie auster, jericho brown, peter balakian, james carroll, jill mccorkle, jacki lyden, jo-ann mort, mitch kaplan, peter ho davies, anne gere, ellen stone, john ayers, cassandra verhaegen, and rachel cohen.

thank you also to the following publications, where some of these poems first appeared:

Arrowsmith: "ways to love and leave you"; "social hour vole"; "attention"; "feel it if"; "the animal question"; "chemical peel"; "airplane landscape, 1992, true story"; "let me be"; and "tenacity"

Jet Fuel Review: "anthrosphere"; "these days i keep falling"; and "sestina for the snake in a man-made lake"

Newcity: "arrhythmia"

Wherever I'm At: An Anthology of Chicago Poetry (Elmwood Park, IL: Chicago Literary Hall of Fame, 2022): "chance, chicago"

finally, everything i make is in conversation with, inspired by, and/or indebted to my parents, ken and judith dewoskin; my in-laws, bill ayers and bernardine dohrn; and the three infinite loves of my life: zayd dohrn, dalin alexi, and light ayli.